MW00878729

Durable Design

Durable Design:

Classical Oration for Speeches and Essays

by Michael J. P. Larson

Minnesota State College – Southeast Technical

Winona, MN

A CreateSpace Book
North Charleston, SC

Copyright © 2012 by Michael Larson
All rights reserved.

ISBN-13: 978-1475087598
ISBN-10: 1475087594

The writing of this book is due in large part to a sabbatical
granted to the author by Minnesota State College –
Southeast Technical.

Table of Contents

Preface   i
Introduction   iii

Part One: Components of Classical Oration
    1. Exordium   3
    2. Narratio   11
    3. Partitio   15
    4. Confirmatio   17
    5. Refutatio   27
    6. Peroratio   31

Part Two: Cohesion and Construction
    1. Thesis   39
    2. Construction Sequence   41
        • Step One: Confirmatio   42
        • Step Two: Confirmatio   45
        • Step Three: Confirmatio   48
        • Step Four: Refutatio   49
        • Step Five: Refutatio   51
        • Step Six: Narratio   52
        • Step Seven: Partitio   53
        • Step Eight: Exordium   54
        • Step Nine: Peroratio   55
        • Step Ten: Transitions   56

Appendix
    Sample Essay   61
    Sample Speech   65

Preface

This is a book about the time-honored art of arranging one's thoughts into a cohesive piece of thesis-driven communication, whether oral or written. The focus, then, is on organization rather than on content or style. The particular method of organization under discussion here is that of *classical oration*, a flexible and robust system for ordering the components of a speech or an essay so as to maximize the rhetorical impact on a given audience.

After a brief introduction, the book is arranged in two parts. The first part defines each of the six components of classical oration, and the second part delineates a suggested sequence for the actual building of a cohesive essay or speech. Included at the end is an appendix containing a sample essay and a sample speech to illustrate classical oration design features.

Lots of people have good ideas but find themselves at a loss when it comes to ordering those ideas in such a way that others can readily apprehend them. This book is for all those people: for speakers and writers—and ultimately for their audiences.

Introduction

Classical oration springs, naturally enough, from the classical tradition in rhetoric, which may be defined as the art of effective communication, and has its roots, as a field of study, in Aristotle's seminal work, *Rhetoric*. A few hundred years after Aristotle, Cicero, the great Roman orator, wrote extensively on rhetorical topics, including the principles of organization. It is in his writing—especially *De inventione* and *De oratore*—that we first see all of the particular components of *classical oration* (as it would come to be known) addressed and examined. Thus the components of classical oration have been studied as such for more than 2000 years and, until modern times, comprised the standard method by which a communicator would organize a thesis-driven speech or essay.

So what are those components? In the simplest terms, they are Aristotle's *beginning*, *middle*, and *end*. The beginning, or introduction, is further broken into three components: a *commencement* (or call to attention), a setting of *context*, and a *preview* of what's to come in the middle. The middle is likewise broken into two components: *proofs* to support one's argument and *refutation* of potential objections to one's argument. And the end is the *conclusion*. So there are six components total in classical oration. Naturally, in classical times and even in the Middle Ages, the components were referred to by their Latin names. The table below gives a visual breakdown of them all, with the Latin terms and their corresponding modern English descriptive phrases. Study this table closely, as it is a summary preview of the entire book.

Components of Classical Oration

Section	Latin Name	Brief English Translation	Description
Beginning or Introduction	*Exordium*	Commencement	That which secures the audience's attention and makes them want to know more
	Narratio	"Back story" or context setting	That which informs the audience of background information necessary to understand fully the middle section
	Partitio	Preview of the parts to come	That which orients the audience to the key arguments they will encounter in the middle section
Middle or Body	*Confirmatio*	"Confirmation" or proofs positive	That which is substantially convincing as to the truth of the communicator's thesis
	Refutatio	Refutation(s) of objections	That which addresses potential objections to the communicator's reasoning
End or Conclusion	*Peroratio*	Conclusion	That which summarizes and leaves the audience with a lasting and persuasive impression

The Principle of Flexibility

For theoretical purposes, it is useful to see all six components separated as they are in the table above. And indeed, it is possible to construct a speech or an essay that follows this structure exactly. But in the practical world of communication, most speeches and essays end up being an approximation of this pattern, and that is perfectly acceptable, depending on each individual combination of topic, thesis, and audience. Any formal, thesis-driven communication is going to commence (exordium) at some point, is going to need some proofs (confirmatio), and is going to conclude (peroratio), so those components at least will always be present. But the other three components—context setting, preview, and refutation—may or may not be present, depending on what is needed for the particular thesis and audience in question.

If it is a highly technical topic to be delivered to a lay audience, then there will likely need to be some context setting (narratio), some defining of key terms, and so on. Conversely, if the audience already has a good understanding of the technical nature of the topic, then the narratio component may be unnecessary and best left out.

In a speech, a preview (partitio) is almost certainly necessary, because the audience does not typically have in front of them the luxury of a text by which they could see for themselves the structure of the whole. Rather, the audience has only the speaker's words to guide them, and those words are gliding by at a constant rate, so it is the speaker's responsibility to help the audience see the structure as much as possible, primarily by way of previews of what's to come and summaries of what has just passed. On the other hand, a short essay (e.g. 2 – 3 pages) may not need a preview, because the whole of the structure is almost constantly in front of the reader already, thus rendering a formal preview superfluous.

Even when all three parts of the beginning are used—exordium, narratio, and partitio—the latter two are sequentially interchangeable. Further, if the back story is a particularly interesting one, it may serve double duty as both narratio and exordium by being the first words, or commencement, of the communication. Therefore, although the exordium, the narratio, and the partitio serve three distinct functions, there are different combinations by which they may introduce one's topic and thesis.

The same can be said of the two sections in the middle, proofs (confirmatio) and refutation (refutatio). Refutation, if it is present at all, may come *before* the proofs, even though in the table above it is listed after. More likely, however, is that proofs of one's own ideas will be intertwined throughout the middle section with refutations of objections to those ideas.

So an important concept for grasping classical oration is this principle of flexibility. That principle, in turn, is tied to an acute awareness of audience. Different pieces of communication and different audiences will require different configurations of the six components. Throughout this text, then, you will see that a consideration of audience is inseparable from the components of organization. Part One will now take a closer look at each component and examine its characteristics.

Part One:

Components of Classical Oration

Exordium: the Commencement

The *exordium* begins with the first sentence of an essay or the first words of a speech. Thus it is the formal act of *commencing* one's communication. There is no set limit as to how long it may go on. In a short essay, it may be only a single paragraph. In a very short essay, it may be a single sentence. Likewise with speeches: depending on what needs to be accomplished, the exordium may be a mere 30 seconds; on the other hand, it may require 5 minutes or more to introduce a very long and complicated message. Most of the time, however, in speeches ranging from 5 – 10 minutes, the exordium lasts less than a minute (and is no longer than two).

Since this component is marked by the very first words in a piece of formal communication, it has a distinctive purpose: it must engage the audience immediately and entice them to continue listening/reading. If it fails in these objectives, if the audience is not interested or engaged, if they have, in a sense, already "checked out," then the rest of the communication stands little chance of being very convincing.

Since the exordium is of such critical importance, rhetoricians have, over the centuries, devised and categorized a number of practical methods for accomplishing both engagement and enticement to continue. What follows is a brief discussion of some of these methods, each considered in relation to a hypothetical thesis:

> *The liberal arts are worthy of study for their own sake, regardless of any practical benefits they may (or may not) impart to the student.*

1. **Broad to narrow.** In this method, sometimes called the *funnel-in* approach, the communicator begins by speaking in very general terms about the topic and narrows the scope eventually to a specific statement of thesis, which ought to be a more pointed expression of the speech's main assertion. Considering our hypothetical thesis, you might begin by speaking broadly of the arts, dividing them into groups of fine arts, servile arts, and liberal arts. Then you might name the seven original liberal arts and talk about how they are representative of other studies that may be classified as liberal arts as well. Then you could mention a few of the practical benefits that come from these liberal arts as a way of leading up to your thesis, which asserts, nevertheless, that the liberal arts are not *dependent* on those practical benefits for their value. Finally, this exordium would conclude with an exact statement of the thesis, as written above.

   One strength of this method is that it is easy to do. It doesn't require much thought; with a little practice, you can almost do it on the fly. If you know your thesis, then you know your topic; if you know your topic, then you can speak in general terms about it. Once you begin speaking generally about it, you simply funnel your way to the clear end-goal of the actual thesis.

So this method is safe and reliable, and it helps to give the audience a big-picture view of the topic, but it can also be a bit boring, a bit predictable, and that is its weakness. Generalities are not usually as interesting as specifics, so in the example above, starting with a broad discussion of "the arts" may lose certain of the audience members immediately.

2. **Questions**. One way to engage the audience is to ask them questions. If the questions are interesting enough, the audience cannot help but try to answer them mentally, and they are thus engaged, whether they meant to be or not. And if the questions are challenging enough, the audience is furthermore enticed into hearing how they might be answered in the remainder of the speech or essay.

Given our thesis, this method of exordium might go as follows: *Do you remember when you were a child and you discovered something new about the world and you wanted to learn everything you could about it—for no other reason than the joy of deepening your knowledge? Maybe it was dinosaurs, or the planets in our solar system, or the legend of King Arthur. Whatever it was for you, do you remember how fun it was to learn? Is it still fun? Or did you get bogged down somewhere in the pressure to make all education practical, something you could use for making money or for contributing to society? What if I told you that there is a branch of knowledge—even for adults—that is akin to the joyful learning you did as a child?*

3. **Quotation.** A quotation can be an effective call to attention as well, depending on the strength of the quotation itself or at least on the reputation of the person being quoted. A strong quotation is thought provoking, elegant, humorous, or some combination of these. If the quotation itself is not particularly strong, then the person being quoted had better be well-admired by the audience. Whether on the strength of the quotation or of the quoted, though, the idea with this method of exordium is the same as any other: engage the audience and entice them to continue with you.

   The following quotation, by John Henry Newman, might work for our hypothetical example: "... there is a Knowledge, which is desirable, though nothing come of it, as being of itself a treasure, and a sufficient remuneration for years of labour." Although some in the audience might be admirers of Cardinal Newman, the real strength here is the gracefulness of the words in their sequence, especially the evocative power of a word like "treasure," and the idea of a Knowledge that might be its own reward for long labors of the mind.

4. **Narration.** Humans love stories. Telling a brief one is, therefore, a good way to engage and entice. A particularly effective use of this method is to begin a story with the exordium but to withhold the ending until the peroratio, or conclusion. In our present example, you might tell the story of a slave

who taught himself secretly to read and, with his new skill, had read a number of great books, loving the knowledge he gleaned from them. And then his secret was discovered and his books taken away. The exordium might end here and the story not be addressed again until the conclusion, when the writer or speaker explains that the taking away of the slave's books did not (indeed, could not) deprive him of the freedom of mind that he had already acquired by way of the knowledge he had gained. Even without his books, he continued to contemplate the truths he had learned, and thus he remained a student of the liberal arts, despite all external appearances.

5. **Shock**. A dramatic way to grab attention is to shock. What if you started like this?

   The liberal arts are worthless! I'm serious. It is not their purpose, after all, to bear fruit. They do not translate into a particular skill set for which someone will pay you handsomely, nor do they necessarily even make you a better person. When you study them, you have at the end no tangible thing to show for it. Absolutely worthless. A waste of time ... unless ... unless, of course, you happen to value knowing truth or recognizing and appreciating beauty or perfecting the intellect and its powers ... and so on.

6. **Challenge**. Sometimes it is possible to secure the audience's attention by issuing a challenge. The key to this method is that the challenge must inspire and not discourage. Consider the following:

Although it is not always an easy path, there is a way for the intellect to be happy. In fact, the intellect, like the body, seeks health, and therein lies its happiness. But as the body, in order to reach its perfection, requires the discipline of good food and consistent exercise, the repeated practice of particular skills, so too the intellect requires the knowledge of truth, the contemplation of beauty, the steady practice of reasoning, in order to reach its potential. And it is the liberal arts that speak to this need.

Here the reader is being challenged to consider the liberal arts as a crucially important discipline that must be adopted in order to achieve the health of one's own intellect.

7. **Intrigue.** Although as we have seen, some of the other methods create intrigue as a matter of course, intrigue may be also be used as a method in its own right, where the entire technique relies on arousing the audience's sense of mystery.

   Although scientists have not invented the machine to take us back in time, time travel is indeed possible. It's called the study of history. Although we are each given only one earthly existence, it is possible to live many lives, to see the world through other lenses and thus understand it better. It's called the study of literature … and so on.

8. **Humor.** Just as humans like stories, they like jokes, which are a type of story; in short, they like to laugh, at least inwardly, and the effect of this

laughter is to relax the mind, even as attention is increased.

Once there was a young man who only liked to surf. All summer he was on the water, and only because his father made him would he go back to school each fall. When he graduated from high school, his father asked him what he was going to do with his life. "Uh. Surf?" replied the young man. "Well, I say you're going to college," said the father. "So if you can find a major for surfing, be my guest." After his first semester at college, the young man was home for Christmas, and he told his father, "Dad? I had to do a lot of research, but I finally found a major that gives me the freedom to perfect my surfing. It's called the Liberal Arts!"

While this list of exordium techniques is not exhaustive, it does give you an idea of how the goals of engagement and enticement might be accomplished. One other consideration regarding the exordium has to do with the communicator's *ethos*. Ethos is an Aristotelian term that refers to the audience's perception of the one who is communicating to them, either by the spoken or the written word. The audience may hold the communicator in low or high regard, or anywhere in between, and Aristotle argues that this view of the communicator, this ethos, has a distinct effect on how well the message is received. A few centuries after Aristotle, Cicero proposes that the most important place to establish one's ethos is in the beginning of one's communication. And this makes perfect sense. The higher regard the audience has for the communicator, the more receptive they will be to what he has to say.

It is good to keep in mind, then, that from the very first sentence of one's speech or essay, the audience is starting to form an opinion of the person behind the words. Some of the methods of exordium will, naturally, have more impact on this than others. For example, if you begin by quoting another, you may be relying on the ethos of the person you are quoting more than your own (and there is nothing wrong with that!). On the other hand, if you attempt to tell a humorous story, then you are relying in large part on your ability to tell it well, whether in writing or in speech. Success would equal a quickly rising ethos, while failure might have the opposite effect.

In any case, ethos is not static. Throughout the speech or essay, it will rise or fall, depending on how the audience perceives the person who is presenting the ideas. Best, of course, as Cicero suggests, is to establish it as well as one can in the introduction, the next stage of which will provide even more opportunity to influence ethos. We turn now to that stage, called *narratio*.

Narratio: the Setting of Context

Narratio literally translates as "story." In an essay or a speech, it is that section, coming after the initial call to attention of the exordium, in which the communicator gives the audience what background information (or "back-story") is necessary to more fully understand the upcoming middle section, where the most important arguments are made. Although it is often useful, the narratio is not an absolutely necessary component in thesis-driven communication. Use it whenever it would benefit your audience's understanding, but don't include it merely out of compulsion.

When, you might ask, is the narratio most beneficial to the audience? Three common scenarios are as follows:

1. *When you need to explain how the issue (the one you are communicating about) came to be what it is.* This is the truest sense of the word, narratio, because it is the telling of a brief story, the story that sets the context for the issue in question. This need arises most often in problem-solution type speeches and papers. The narratio gives witness to the existence of the problem, in case the audience was unaware of it,

and the middle section examines more closely the causes of the problem as well as argues for a particular solution—often a new policy or law.

Example. Let's say you are alarmed by the issue of illegal immigration and you want to propose some tighter controls against it. The function of the narratio, in this case, would be to give the audience a brief history of illegal immigration in this country, probably some statistics to show the trends, some tracing of how policies have evolved to their current state, just enough information to establish in the audience's mind that the problem is real and needs some attention. (Not until the middle section—the *confirmatio* and *refutatio*—would you expound on aspects such as *why* you believe illegal immigration to be a danger in the first place, *why* the present policies are not working and therefore *why*, in your opinion, they need to be changed, as well as *what* those changes need to be.)

2. *When you need to explain concepts or key terms that your audience should understand in order to fully grasp your argument(s).* If you want to argue that the best chess opening to play is the Ruy Lopez, then you must first explain to your audience what a chess opening is. And depending on their familiarity with chess in general, you may even have to give them a brief overview of the rules and the object of the game. In short, the narratio serves to bring your

audience "up to speed" with technical information so that they are not lost when you present the main arguments.

3. *When you need to make sure that your audience understands a common word in the particular way that you mean it to be understood.* For instance, if you are going to use the word, "love," frequently, you might want to take a moment to specify your particular meaning, since it is used in our culture in so many different ways: romantic feelings between a couple; affections for anything we happen to like: a friend, a bowl of ice cream, a walk in the park, etc.; simple acts of kindness toward others, be they people, animals, plants, etc.; a long-term state of commitment to another; the attempt to please God, and so on. Clearly the word, "love," gets assigned to all of these things, yet they couldn't be more different from one another in essence. Thus it is important that the communicator specify the particular use for the present speech or essay. This may be done positively ("This is how I am using the word...") or negatively ("Now, by 'love' I do not mean ___, nor do I mean ___, nor do I even mean ___. What I do mean is ___.").

Ethos Establishment

It should be noted here as well that, just as with the exordium, the narratio continues to impact the communicator's ethos. And this makes sense if you think about it. If a speaker or a writer takes the time to prepare you properly for full understanding, then your view of him goes up. You naturally appreciate his willingness to help you along. You also probably estimate his competence in the topic as being fairly high, based not only on his ability to explain preliminary material but also on his awareness that it would need explaining at all. In short, trust increases to the degree that the narratio is handled well.

In contrast, consider how you feel when someone jumps right into a difficult topic, speaks over your head, and leaves you "in the dust," so to speak. In such a case, ethos will decline, and the effectiveness of the overall communication with it.

As with the exordium, the narratio has no set length, but it should be generally proportionate to the length of the whole of the communication. In a 10-page paper, for instance, a full page of narratio would not be out of line. Likewise, in a 10-minute speech, spending a minute or so on narratio would seem appropriate. These examples are not meant to propose that the narratio should always be exactly 10% of the total length; rather, they are meant merely to give a rough perspective in relation to the whole. In practice, depending on what needs to be accomplished in the narratio for a given speech or paper, the length of it could vary considerably.

Partitio: the Division of Parts

Partitio is close in letters and in concept to our modern word, "partition." Applied to classical oration, it refers to the partitioning, or division, of parts found in the body of the speech or essay. Specifically, it is the revealing of those parts to the audience so that, by anticipating what is coming, they may understand it better when it comes. As you might expect, the partitio, just like the other components of the introduction (exordium and narratio), has the potential to help build ethos. If the audience sees that the communicator has considered the topic carefully and developed a clear design for its presentation, there is naturally a higher degree of confidence and trust in that person to deliver something of value.

In speeches, the partitio is almost always a good idea, as the audience does not have a written record of the material, so they are entirely dependent on the speaker's words as a means of following the flow and structure of the speech. A preview of what is to come aids them in that task.

In essays, a preview is less vital because the audience (the reader) has access to the structure by way of the written text itself. Still, a preview is often helpful, especially in longer essays, because once again the reader is aided by the ability to foresee the design of what is to come. With that map in one's head, it is much easier to follow the flow of thought as the writer intended it.

Whether in an essay or a speech, the partitio typically comes after the narratio (if there is one) and before the middle section, which is the section being previewed. It is certainly possible, however, to place it *before* the narratio, in which case the narratio itself would be previewed as well.

Of the six components in classical oration, the partitio is the briefest, often consisting of only a sentence or two. Here is a sample partitio for a speech that argues, in its middle section, for the advantages of herbalism over conventional medicine: *In the next few minutes, I'll be showing you the fundamental clash of philosophies between conventional medicine, which tries to control disease by high-powered external agents such as prescription drugs or surgery; and herbalism, which tries to eradicate disease from the inside out by stimulating the body's own immune response. After exploring this basic difference, I'll talk about a couple of common but dangerous side effects from the conventional approach. And finally, I'll address two popular misconceptions regarding applied herbalism: that herbs are not potent enough to be effective as medicine, and that their medicinal use has no basis in science.*

It's as simple as that. Obviously, a longer speech or a complicated essay may have more partitions to preview, but the principle is the same: give the audience a "roadmap" by which they have some sense of how you will proceed.

Confirmatio: the Positive Proofs

The heart of classical oration is the *confirmatio*. It is here that the communicator's argument is confirmed, or proven. In other words, the confirmatio gives the *reasons* why the communicator's thesis is true, and therefore why it ought to be believed and/or acted upon. Although the components of the introduction—exordium, narratio, and partitio—are important for engaging the audience's interest and helping them to understand what is to come, the confirmatio is the actual substance of the communication.

Just as the exordium has different methods of achieving its purpose (to engage and entice), so too the confirmatio has specific means by which it gives proof to the thesis. These are *inductive reasoning*, *deductive reasoning*, and *testimony*. While this text is not meant to be a guidebook for developing content, it will be useful here to explain briefly the nature of these tools of confirmation. The second part of this book will take a look at some of the practical methods of organizing these three types of proofs.

Inductive Reasoning

Inductive reasoning takes particular observations and uses them to arrive at general theories. In rhetorical communication, a thesis is usually a kind of general theory about something. The use of inductive reasoning, then, would involve revealing to the audience some observations that, taken together, could reasonably lead one to affirm the theory contained in the thesis, or if not in the thesis itself, then in some subordinate point that must be established on the way to proving the thesis. Aristotle referred to these revealed observations in the inductive process as *examples*, and these can be broken down into several different types.

1. *Common.* Using, as an illustration of the point you are trying to make, something—an event, a common occurrence, a relatively famous person, etc.—that is well-known among the audience.

2. *Educational.* An example that springs from a body of knowledge with which the communicator is familiar but the audience is not. (e.g. A literature professor might describe a particular scene from a play of Shakespeare to illustrate his point. Or a trial lawyer might outline the details of a prior case to establish a precedent example for the jury.)

3. *Personal.* Using something from personal experience—a person you know, something you witnessed, something that happened to you, etc.—to illustrate the truth of your assertion.

4. *Hypothetical.* Making up a scenario that the audience understands to be not actually true but certainly plausible enough and thereby convincing in its own right.

5. *Analogical.* An example by way of comparison. (e.g. If your point is that human society functions best when hierarchies are clear, you might refer to the wolf pack and how their very survival depends on every member of the pack understanding its individual rank within the whole.)

6. *Statistical.* This is an example by way of the testimony of some other source, someone who has collected and published data, which represents a bundle of examples distilled into a single number or set of numbers.

Each of these example types is itself an example of the use of inductive reasoning to support an assertion. In effect, you say, "Look here, my point is true because I can show you another circumstance with similar (or analogical) parameters that yields the same result."

Deductive Reasoning

A second type of proof that may be used in the confirmatio is that of deductive reasoning. Instead of moving from particular observations to form general theories, as induction does, deduction moves from combining generally accepted propositions to form absolutely certain conclusions. The formal technique for deductive reasoning is the *syllogism.* Although this is not a text in formal logic, we will take a brief look at three common types of syllogisms: the *categorical,* the *hypothetical,* and the *disjunctive.*

1. **Categorical**.

- Businesses that do not show loyalty to their employees create an unstable working environment.
- Modern NBA teams do not show loyalty to many of their players.
- Therefore, modern NBA teams create an unstable working environment.

The formal structure of a syllogism is, as shown here, two *premises* (the first two statements) followed by an inevitable *conclusion* (the third statement). Here we see a large category established first: businesses that do not show loyalty to their employees. Then a smaller group—modern NBA teams—is placed within that larger category. If both of the first two statements are true, then the conclusion follows automatically and absolutely—because what is true for the larger category (the creation of an unstable working environment) must by necessity be true for those contained within the larger category—in this case, modern NBA teams.

2. **Hypothetical**.

- If a business does not show loyalty to its employees, then the working environment will be unstable.
- Modern NBA teams do not show loyalty to many of their players.
- Therefore, the working environment for modern NBA teams is unstable.

Hypothetical syllogisms always use an *if/then* structure to set up the logical relationship. The "if" part of the statement is called the *antecedent*, and the "then" part is called the *consequent*. In this syllogism, the if/then statement comes first; then the second statement shows a particular instance of the "if" part of the initial statement. This is called *affirming the antecedent*. Once again, the conclusion must follow, provided that both of the prior statements are true.

Besides affirming the antecedent, hypothetical syllogisms may also proceed by showing an instance where the "then" part has *not* occurred (called *denying the consequent*) and thereby still reach a certain conclusion, as follows:

- If a business does not show loyalty to its employees, then the working environment will be unstable.
- The working environment at Joe's Pub is stable.
- Therefore, Joe's Pub is not disloyal to its employees.

3. **Disjunctive**.

Disjunctive syllogisms use an either/or structure to set up the logical relationship. If a situation is either A or B, the logical implications are several. If we know it is A, then we can deduce that it is also *not* B. Alternatively, if we know it is B, we can deduce that it is also *not* A. Furthermore, if we know that it is *not* A or that it is *not* B, then we can deduce in each case that it *is* the other. What follows are four examples that correspond to each type of disjunctive syllogism just described.

- Everyone is either introverted or extroverted.
- We know John is introverted.
- Therefore, he is not extroverted.

- Everyone is either introverted or extroverted.
- We know Maria is extroverted.
- Therefore, she is not introverted.

- Everyone is either introverted or extroverted.
- We know John is not extroverted.
- Therefore, he is introverted.

- Everyone is either introverted or extroverted.
- We know Maria is not introverted.
- Therefore, she is extroverted.

Formal syllogisms, such as those given above, find their proper place in the study of logic, which is a branch of philosophy. In rhetoric, which is our focus in this text, deductive thought is rarely expressed as a formal syllogism. Instead, communicators will often reveal deduction by way of the *enthymeme*, which is merely a truncated syllogism. Instead of three formal statements, as in the examples above, an enthymeme uses only one or two of the statements in such a way that the rest of the syllogism is implied. What follows are sample enthymeme versions of the syllogisms exemplified above, beginning with the categorical.

- It's clear that NBA teams do not show much loyalty to many of their players, and it's also obvious that businesses who do not show loyalty to their employees end up creating unstable working environments. (conclusion is implied but not actually stated: *that NBA teams have unstable working environments*)

- Let's face it: NBA teams do not have a very stable working environment. And why would they, since they do not show most of their players much loyalty? (one of the premises is implied: *that businesses who do not show employee loyalty create unstable working environments*)

- We know that Joe's Pub is not disloyal to its employees, because the working environment there is quite stable according to those same employees. (one of the premises is implied: *that businesses who are disloyal to employees will not have stable working environments*)

- People are either introverts or extroverts. And we know John's not an extrovert. (the conclusion is implied: *that John is an introvert*)

- People are either introverts or extroverts, and that's all I need to say about Maria. (One of the premises and the conclusion are implied. The assumption here is that the audience knows enough about Maria to know *that she **is** an extrovert*—and the conclusion naturally follows *that she is **not** an introvert*.)

Enthymemes are used frequently in rhetoric to establish both minor and major points throughout the communication. What's important to recognize about them is that there is a formal, syllogistic thought process behind them, even though certain parts of the syllogism are only implied when expressed as an enthymeme.

Testimony

The third means by which a thesis may be proven is the *testimony* of someone other than the communicator. Usually this testimony is that of an expert, someone who is recognized (or could be, once you make his credentials known) in the field you are discussing. In other words, this is an appeal to *authority* rather than to logical reasoning— either inductive or deductive. The effectiveness of this appeal depends on how much the audience trusts and respects the opinion and the words of the source being referenced. In other words, what is the ethos of that source in the eyes of this particular audience? If your topic explores the risks involved with open heart surgery, then the opinions and comments of a cardiologist might go quite a ways toward supporting (i.e. "proving") a particular point you are trying to make.

The proof of testimony, then, can be a solid one. Sometimes we believe something simply because we trust completely the person who says it is true. In fact, much of what we believe most sincerely, we believe for this reason. How many of us, for instance, have proved for ourselves, either inductively or deductively, that the Earth is spherical rather than planar? Yet we do not doubt it, and this is because we trust those who *have* gone through the proofs to be telling us the truth.

───────────────────

In reality, any of the three types of proofs contained in the confirmatio can be used well or poorly. If our examples are apt and vivid, then our inductive reasoning is solid. But if our examples are not accurate representations or are uninteresting, then our inductive reasoning is weak. If our enthymemes have the clear logic of syllogistic thought behind them, then our deductive reasoning is solid. But if our enthymemes imply conclusions that, upon closer examination, are illogical or unproven, or if the premises themselves are false, then our deductive reasoning is weak. If our appeals to authority are legitimate and well-chosen, then our use of testimony is solid. But if our appeals to authority do not induce confidence in the audience, then our use of testimony is a weak proof indeed.

It should be noted here as well that there is no standard requirement as to the balance of proofs you must use. You may use all three—inductive, deductive, and testimonial—or any combination of one or two of them. Furthermore, you may use any number of particular proofs within one type. For instance, you might use three or four examples (all inductive proofs) that illustrate the same point. Ultimately it is up to the individual communicator to determine which and how many proofs are necessary, given time or length constraints, to convince the audience that one's thesis is true.

Refutatio: Refutation of Objections

Sometimes it is necessary to refute anticipated objections to your arguments. In classical oration, this is called the *refutatio*. Like the confirmatio, it is a kind of proof for your thesis and thus belongs in the middle section of a speech or essay. However, instead of presenting a positive argument as the confirmatio does, the refutatio shows why an opposing view is flawed. Since it is reactive rather than active, method in refutation is best understood by examining once again the tools of confirmatio: inductive reasoning, deductive reasoning, and testimony. The anticipated objections to your arguments are each going to fall under one of these categories.

Let's say your thesis is that studying and practicing a musical instrument develops character and intellect. One of your inductive proofs might be a statistical study that shows a higher likelihood of finishing college among those who studied an instrument in childhood than among those who did not. You anticipate that some in the audience might think to themselves that there are probably more people with college degrees who did not study an instrument in childhood than there are who did. In order to refute this anticipated objection, you need to reiterate that it is a higher *percentage*—not a higher number of total people. In other words, of those who studied an instrument, 72% finish college, whereas of those who did not study an instrument, only 41% finish college (or whatever it is—these numbers are made up for this example, but you get the idea …). And it is the percentage figure, not the total numbers, that would support the thesis statement in this case.

With regard to deductive reasoning, refutation usually involves pointing out the logical flaw in the opposing viewpoint. The logical structure of the above thesis might have underlying it the following two syllogisms.

- Serious study of anything develops the intellect.
- Taking up an instrument requires serious study of it.
- Therefore, taking up an instrument develops the intellect.

- Disciplined practice of any skill over a long period of time develops character.
- Taking up an instrument requires disciplined practice over a long period of time.
- Therefore, taking up an instrument develops character.

The beautiful thing about deductive reasoning is that if premises are true and the argument is properly constructed, the conclusion is absolutely certain. Objections then are usually at the level of the premises. In the first syllogism, it would be hard for anyone to disagree with the first premise, that serious study develops the intellect; however, some might disagree with the notion that learning an instrument requires serious study of either music in general or the specific instrument's qualities in particular. And if they do not accept the second premise, then they need not accept the conclusion either.

A counter to this anticipated objection might be a clarification of what is meant by the study of an instrument. You might say, in effect, "I'm not talking about those who pick up an instrument and play by ear or by instinct, for indeed, they do not *study* either music or instrumentation in the way that I mean. Rather, I am referring to the student who has an expert teacher and regular lessons over a long period of time."

Another area for possible objections and refutations in the realm of deductive reasoning is that of logical fallacies, which are well beyond the scope of this text. Suffice it to say that proving an argument often involves the exposing of faulty reasoning (i.e. a fallacy) in the opposing viewpoint—a true form of refutation.

Finally, objections to arguments that appeal to authority (i.e. testimonial proofs) have generally to do with the ethos of that authority. If the source you reference is not well-respected by your audience, then they will object to your point on that basis. To refute such an objection would require a bit of re-education regarding the competency and the character of the authority in question. In other words, if you anticipate that the authority you are using is not held in high regard (but ought to be), then you must take the time to help your audience see this person in the right light. If you are successful in this, then the objection to the proof disappears.

Whether you are dealing with objections rooted in induction, deduction, or testimony, refutation can be an important part of the overall communication. Unlike the confirmatio, however, it is not a required component. If there are no anticipated objections, then there is no reason to refute imaginary ones. In fact, this would only serve to confuse your audience (and likely undermine your argument). Nevertheless, if you do use some refutation in your speech or essay, it does not necessarily have to follow the confirmatio as a separate section. More natural would be to intermingle the two. You make a point (confirmatio); you see an objection to that point and deal with it on the spot (refutatio); then you make another point, and so on. Still another arrangement might be to have the refutatio first, before the confirmatio. This might be an especially effective method when the objections you anticipate are commonly held and seemingly powerful. By dealing with them first, you clear the air for your audience to accept more willingly the confirmatio.

Peroratio: the Conclusion

The *peroratio,* or conclusion, is an important component in classical oration. It begins when the body of the essay or speech is completed, and it ends with the last word of the last sentence. The primary purpose of the peroratio is to make a lasting and favorable impression on the audience. This can be accomplished in a number of ways.

1. **Summary**. A traditionally favorite way to finish is to summarize what you have just covered in the body of the communication. Although it never hurts, there are two situations in which a summary makes especially good sense:
   a. *In a long or complicated essay.* Even though readers hold the text in their hands and therefore can refer to its prior parts whenever they choose, a summary is a great help for them in organizing the main points in their minds. After all, in a long or complicated essay, they have likely just been immersed in a great many details and therefore may have lost sight of the larger picture. A concise summary helps them to

regain this perspective while it also encourages retention of the subject matter.

b. *In any speech.* For the same reason that speeches should always include the partitio (a preview, at the end of the introduction, of what is to come), they should also include a summary in the conclusion. The audience of a speech—even a relatively short one—does not have the luxury of referring to a text to see the organizational structure. They must rely completely on the speaker's words to guide them through the whole of the communication he offers. Previews and summaries help with this task of enabling the audience to follow the flow of thought, to see how it is organized, and to remember it after the speech is over.

2. **Any of the methods of exordium.** Interestingly, the methods of beginnings are often effective as endings, too. The section on exordium has covered these in more detail, but I will include the list here as a reminder, with notes where necessary to differentiate between their uses at the beginning and at the end.

a. *Broad to narrow.* In a conclusion, this one gets reversed (i.e. Narrow to broad). Instead of moving from a broad view of the topic to a focused and particular thesis, you start the conclusion by rephrasing the thesis first and then move toward a statement of the general principles that led you to form your thesis. Often this process is like a reverse-order syllogism: start with the syllogism's conclusion and finish by revealing the major premise, which is usually a kind of general principle. For example, if your thesis is that seat belt laws should be kept as they are, you might move from that particular assertion to a statement about the purpose of law in general, which is to protect the common good.

b. *Questions.* Questions in the conclusion differ slightly from those in the introduction. In the introduction, questions are meant to create curiosity, to intrigue. In the conclusions, questions are rhetorical. They are asked in such a way that the answer is now obvious and reaffirms what has been communicated in the confirmatio and refutatio.

c. *Quotations.* As with the introduction, quotations in the conclusion should be thought-provoking and elegant, and the source should not be someone against whom the audience has a bias.

d. *Narration.* As the section on exordium mentions, narration often involves the beginning of a story in the introduction, a suspension of that story through the middle section, and the story's end, naturally enough, in the conclusion. This technique creates a full-circle effect for the whole of the communication.

e. *Shock.* This is less likely to be used in the conclusion but still possible if the shocking statement is a revelation of something that makes sense of the whole. For instance, someone who argues against abortion might reveal in the conclusion that her mother had seriously considered aborting her but had (obviously) decided not to go through with it.

f. *Challenge.* This is a common way to conclude if the argument calls for action and not just belief or understanding. The writer or speaker challenges the audience to take the next step in whatever action he has been advocating.

g. *Intrigue.* Intrigue is more likely to be an introductory technique since, almost by definition, it accomplishes the exordium's purpose (to engage and entice). It is, however, a possible conclusion as well—especially, for example, with conspiratorial topics (e.g. "So as you can see, there are several good reasons to doubt the official explanation regarding the assassination of Mr. Kennedy. Surely a better explanation lies waiting to be uncovered...")

h. *Humor.* For some topics, especially light ones, a humorous conclusion might work, but it is normally more effective as an introductory technique.

As is the case with the exordium, combinations of these techniques are also possible in the peroratio. Especially common is to give a brief summary followed by one of the other techniques described here. In any case, the conclusion should not go on for long: a paragraph in a short essay, perhaps a few paragraphs in a long essay, less than a minute in a short speech, and no more than a few minutes in a long speech.

Establishment of Pathos

According to Cicero, just as the introduction is the proper place to establish ethos, so the conclusion is the best place to make use of *pathos*. Aristotle defined pathos as the communicator's appeal(s) to the emotions of the audience. Despite their prevalence in the worlds of advertising, show business, and politics, emotional appeals do not make good arguments. Nevertheless, *after* the argument has been reasonably made in the confirmatio (and perhaps the refutatio), it is perfectly legitimate to intensify the audience's response with an emotional appeal, for it is in the emotions that we carry our feelings, and feelings stay with us sometimes in a more powerful way than knowledge or intellectual understanding does.

The use of pathos is not a separate act in and of itself but may be merely an aspect of one of the concluding techniques. For instance, a narrative technique might evoke pity or indignation; a quotation might inspire; the use of shock might cause fear; and so on. In any case, the idea would be to use emotion in the service of something higher—namely the intellect, which ought to be grounded in truth and which ought to have been satisfied by the proofs and refutation offered in the middle section of the speech or essay.

Part Two:

Cohesion and Construction

Thesis as Organizing Principle

Once you understand the components of classical oration, you need a method, a system by which you can put them all together into a cohesive essay or speech. Cohesion is the unifying principle behind the act of organization, and in rhetoric—whether oral or written—cohesion finds its source in a well-designed thesis statement. All order, in every aspect of the overall communication, springs from this small but powerful element.

You might ask, what makes a good thesis statement? Consider the following equation:

Thesis = Topic + Assertion (*about* the topic)

Let's say your topic is *music*. The concept of music, by itself, is NOT a thesis. In order to make it so, you must say something *about* it: "Music is good." Okay. Now you have a thesis, but it's weak. It's weak because it's vague. What kind of music? And what specifically is meant by *good*? Try again. "Classical music is good because it is melodically complex." Much better. You might still ask yourself, Is *all* classical music melodically complex? If not, then further specification is needed. Is melodic complexity always a good thing? If not, then further refinement, once again, will be needed. After some more tweaking, you might arrive at something like the following: "Classical music stands the test of time in part because of its melodic complexity." In fact, a thesis may be tweaked as necessary all throughout the drafting process, but the above assertion has at least the minimum qualities needed to begin building and organizing a speech or an essay around it.

In addition to its being your most important point, the thesis statement is the key to *how* you will organize your thoughts. Every component of classical oration should relate in some way back to it. In your thesis, for example, is an implied structure for the confirmatio. Likewise, in anticipated objections to your thesis are potential points to be refuted (the refutatio). Furthermore, how those proofs of the middle section are constructed will suggest the best introductory and concluding components as well. In short, if you want your essay or speech to be a unified whole and not simply a collection of plug-in parts, then look to a clearly conceived and well-worded thesis statement to provide that cohesion.

The following pages of this book will walk you through the steps of organization, using the thesis statement as the ordering principle behind each component of classical oration.

Construction Sequence

Once you have a good working thesis, you can begin the organizational design of your essay or speech. The following sequence is a step-by-step method for accomplishing that process.

Step One	Discover the implied structure of the argument.	*Confirmatio*
Step Two	Choose specific proofs and develop them.	*Confirmatio*
Step Three	Choose an order for the proofs.	*Confirmatio*
Step Four	Consider objections to the proofs.	*Refutatio*
Step Five	If necessary, place refutations in appropriate slots.	*Refutatio*
Step Six	Determine necessary background information.	*Narratio*
Step Seven	Write the preview.	*Partitio*
Step Eight	Choose and write a commencement.	*Exordium*
Step Nine	Choose and write a conclusion.	*Peroratio*
Step Ten	Create smooth transitions between all sections.	

As you can see, the first five steps have to do with organizing the "body" section of the communication. Although the introduction comes first in the final presentation, it does not make sense to write it until you know more clearly what you are actually introducing. So the body is developed first (Steps 1 – 5). Then the next three steps have to do with the introduction. Step nine is the conclusion, and step ten is the finishing touches of the organization process: applying transitions within and between the sections. What follows is a more detailed account of each step.

Step One: *Discover the implied structure of the argument (confirmatio).*

Behind your thesis statement is a reasoning process—however good or bad—that causes you to assert whatever it is you are asserting. Discovering and examining this reasoning process will give you a good idea as to how the body of your speech or essay might be organized. Suppose your thesis statement is this:

> *Reading the great works of literature is an excellent education for life.*

What really is being communicated in such a thesis? What is the underlying reasoning that allows the assertion to be made? To help us determine this, imagine the thesis to be an enthymeme (i.e. a truncated syllogism). If we were to expand this enthymeme into a full syllogism, it might look something like this:

- Reading the great works of literature gives one deep insight into human nature.
- Deep insight into human nature enables one to live well.
- Therefore, reading the great works of literature is an excellent education for life.

In this syllogism lies the basic structure of deductive reasoning behind the thesis. In order to convince the audience that the conclusion is true, you need to convince them first that the premises are true, for if they are, then the conclusion follows automatically (provided you have constructed the underlying syllogism properly). This fact suggests an initial structure for the confirmatio, the proofs positive: divide it into two basic parts, one each to prove the two premises.

Let's look again at the first premise: *Reading the great works of literature gives one deep insight into human nature.* Why should your audience believe this to be true? Well, they might very well be convinced by some inductive reasoning (i.e. examples that illustrate the truth of the assertion). Perhaps you could choose three or four famous characters from great works of literature and describe briefly how, in each case, the author makes clear some important aspect of human nature through the particular character in question. If your examples are well-chosen, and if you explain them vividly, then your audience will likely accept the premise as true, and you will thus be half way toward proving your thesis to be true as well.

Now, how about the second premise? *Deep insight into human nature enables one to live well.* Here, you might ask yourself some questions: What are the real goals of education? A well-lived life, perhaps? If so, what constitutes a well-lived life? Would such a life be dependent, at least in part, on an understanding of oneself as well as one's neighbor (i.e. human nature)? If so, you might have the makings of another underlying syllogism:

- The end goal of education is a well-lived life.
- A well-lived life requires a deep understanding of human nature.
- Therefore, an excellent education will deepen one's understanding of human nature.

Here again, the premises will need to be proved in order to ensure the audience's acceptance of the conclusion, but you can start to see here how one piece of reasoning might be dependent on another. So far, then, the structure of the confirmatio is taking shape as follows:

1. Establish that reading great works of literature can give one this deep understanding of human nature.
   a. Use a few well-chosen examples from great works of literature that allow the reader to gain valuable insight into human nature.
      i. Example one
      ii. Example two
      iii. Example three

2. Establish that an important component of a strong education is a deep understanding of human nature.

    a. Establish that the general purpose of education is to improve one's ability to live well.
        i. Use a quotation to this effect from a highly respected source
    b. Establish that living well requires a deep understanding of human nature.
        i. Use a personal or hypothetical example that illustrates some negative results that flow from ignorance regarding human nature.

The main thing to remember in this first step is that the thesis itself is the organizing principle, that there is some kind of reasoning process behind it, that this reasoning process should be discovered by the writer or speaker, and then translated and articulated to the audience so that they might understand why they should agree with the assertion contained in the thesis. That is what effective communication is all about.

Step Two: *Choose specific proofs and develop them (confirmatio).*

Once you have the basic structure for the proofs in mind, you can go about the task of choosing particular examples, of working out the specific wording you will use to show any deductive reasoning, of choosing the exact quotation(s) or other appeals to authority, and so on. In the case of our sample thesis and the outline we have so far constructed, the process might unfold as follows:

1. How does someone gain a deep understanding of human nature? One sure way is by the close study of great literature.

    a. In Shakespeare's *Hamlet*, we learn about the human capacity for betrayal motivated by ambition, about the desire for justice coupled with the temptation to avenge, about the strength of loyalty, about the pain of grief, about the paralysis between duty and fear, about deception, about madness in the face of abandonment, about spiritual instinct, as well as a host of other aspects of human nature.

    b. In Cervantes's Don Quixote, we learn about the human capacity for delusion, for innocence and ignorance, for romanticism, and so on.

    c. In Homer's *Odyssey*, we learn of the human capacity for cunning, the instinct for home and homewardness, the desire for glory, the distraction of pleasure, the contrast of fidelity and infidelity, the suddenness of violence and vengeance, and so on.

2. Establish that a key outcome of a strong education is a deepened understanding of human nature.

    a. In speaking about the recipient of a good liberal arts education, John Henry Newman writes, "He profits by an intellectual tradition, [...] He apprehends the great outlines of knowledge, the principles on which it rests, the scale of its parts, its lights and its shades, its great points and its little, as he cannot otherwise apprehend them. Hence it is that his education is called 'Liberal.' A habit of mind is formed which lasts through life, of which the attributes are, freedom, equitableness, calmness, moderation, and wisdom."[1]

b. But it would be impossible to live as Newman describes without a deep understanding of human nature. Imagine, for instance, a man who ignores human nature, both in himself and in others. He remains ignorant of how his actions affect those around him, of his own motivations, of the motivations of others, and so on. His life is marked by impulsive behaviors, by a kind of slavery to his whims, by failed relationships, by an inconsistency of actions, in short by foolishness. Quite the opposite of the characteristics described by Newman.

In each example, more detail might be given by the writer or speaker than I have given here. How much detail will be determined by the length requirements of the writing or speaking situation and by the audience's assumed knowledge going into that situation. The point in

---

[1] John Henry Newman, *The Idea of a University* (Notre Dame: Notre Dame University Press, 1990), 76.

this present text, however, is not to produce content so much as it is to show design in the act of construction and sequencing.

Step Three: *Choose an order for the proofs (confirmatio).*

Once you have assembled some specific proofs, you must choose an order by which to present them in your speech or paper. In our sample construction, it can be argued that it makes sense to first establish that a key outcome of a good education is a deepened understanding of human nature before attempting to show that the great works of literature can provide this deepened understanding. The sequence then would be as follows:

1. Newman quotation

2. Hypothetical example of the man without an understanding of human nature and how he can be contrasted with Newman's description.

3. Illustrative examples of some great works of literature that can impart a deepened understanding of human nature. (Chronological arrangement)
    a. *The Odyssey*
    b. *Don Quixote*
    c. *Hamlet*

Step Four: *Consider objections to the proofs (refutatio).*

In considering objections that others might have to your proofs, you should simply start with the first proof and put yourself in some skeptical shoes for a few minutes. Then do the same for the second proof, and so on.

1. Regarding the Newman quotation, since the Cardinal is not a household name in contemporary society, an audience might object that they know nothing about him and therefore have no particular reason to heed what he says. This objection is easily met by briefly mentioning his credentials, by placing him appropriately in his historical context, before the quotation is used, something to the effect of "John Henry Newman was not only a Cardinal of the Catholic Church but also a leading 19th-century voice in the field of education. His lectures-made-into-a-book, *The Idea of a University*, is one of the most enduring of masterpieces in the field."

2. Objections to the hypothetical example of a man who does not have an understanding of human nature would depend on how well this hypothetical man is described. If you pull out characteristics from certain types of behaviors you have observed over and over in life, then chances are good that you will be resonating with your audience's experiences as well. In hypothetical examples, it is especially important to choose *universal* traits—those that are likely

to be familiar to a large share of your audience, thus reducing any cause for objection.

3. A possible objection to the examples from literature is that some people—maybe even most—learn better by simply living their own experience than by reading about the experience of others. Refutation of this objection might be met in a couple of different ways:

   a. First, you could explain that this is the very problem with insufficient education. If students are not given a good, foundational education in the early part of their lives, then they will not have learned *how* to learn vicariously (e.g. by books) and will be limited in their future lives to learning via experience only.

   b. Second, the problems with learning being restricted to experience alone are threefold:

      i. It can be very costly. In order for the learning to take place, people (including oneself) might have to get hurt: physically, emotionally, financially, and so on.

      ii. It is quite limiting in scope. In experiential learning, what can be learned is restricted to one's own experiences. In the soaking up of great literature, by contrast, there is practically no limit to what can be learned—about

> human nature, to be sure, and
> about a wide range of other
> topics as well.
>
> iii. It is slow. Experiential learning
> proceeds at the speed of one life.
> In vicarious learning through
> literature, a lifetime of learning
> may be acquired, in some sense,
> in a week or two.

Finally, you might concede that experiential learning is indeed a good in and of itself, as far as it goes, and that some people get along just fine by this method alone. Nevertheless, an education beyond one's own experiences can be both broadening and deepening, and that is one of the advantages offered by the reading of great works of literature.

Step Five: *Place refutations in appropriate slots (refutatio).*

Once you have considered what objections there might be to your proofs and how you will refute those objections, then you will want to place them in the appropriate slots. Remember that refutations can come as their own section—refutatio—or intermixed with the proofs. After adding in refutations, our current project might look like this:

1. Proof. Newman quotation, with establishment of his credentials.

2. Proof. Hypothetical example of a man who does not understand human nature:
   a. Failed relationships.
   b. Repeated impulsive actions.
   c. Contrasted with Newman's description of a well-educated person.

3. Proofs. Examples from great literature.
   a. Homer
   b. Cervantes
   c. Shakespeare

4. Refutation. Objection: experience is a good enough teacher.
   a. Experiential learning can be costly
      i. Financially
      ii. Physically
      iii. Emotionally
   b. Experiential learning is limited in scope.
   c. Experiential learning is slow.
   d. Concession: Experiential learning is good as far as it goes. But we also have the capacity for learning so much more.

Step Six: *Determine necessary background information (narratio).*

This step pertains to the development of the *narratio*. Now that you know more concretely what the middle section of your speech or essay looks like, you will want to ask yourself, "What does my audience need to know in the way of background information in order to fully understand what I am going to reveal to them in the main part of my argument?" A good place to start in determining an answer to this question is to consider key terms. What important words will you be using, and might they be misunderstood if you don't clarify your use of them at the beginning?

In our ongoing sample project, a term like "liberal arts" might be a good candidate for further explanation. You might say something like this: "When I speak of education in this context, I am referring specifically to an education in the liberal arts. And by liberal arts, I do not mean *liberal* in the political or moral sense. Rather, I mean it in its traditional educational sense, as in the seven liberal arts, the study of which has the effect of *liberating* the mind of the student by increasing its powers to reason, to understand, and to communicate well what is understood. And specifically, within the liberal arts, I will be discussing the discipline of literature and how the study of it deepens one's understanding of human nature."

In this case, the above might be all that is necessary for the narratio; in another speech or paper, you may have quite a bit of background material to cover. It all depends on how technical or obscure the topic is and how much the audience is assumed to know about it coming in.

Step Seven: *Write the preview (partitio).*

The preview is nothing more than a brief statement of what's to come in the body of the speech or essay. For example, *We'll take a look at what is meant by a good education in general and at how the lack of it might cause some extra difficulties in life. Then we'll take a closer look at some specific examples from literature that illustrate its value as a method by which we can become well educated. Finally, I will address the notion that "book learning" is not really necessary, the idea that experience alone can make us equally well educated.*

As you can see, just the main points of the body outline are mentioned, enough to give the audience a sense of direction and an anticipation of the arguments.

Step Eight: *Choose and write a commencement (exordium).*

The particular technique of commencement should be chosen in light of the speech or essay you have so far constructed. You should be asking yourself, "Given where I mean to take my audience, how best might I both engage them and entice them to want more of what I have to say?" Using the exordium technique of *intrigue*, we might try to engage our audience initially as follows:

Although we are each given only one earthly existence, I am here to say that it is possible nonetheless to live many lives, to see the world through multiple lenses and thus to understand it—and ourselves—better. Despite the fact that truth itself is one, there are many ways of finding it, many roads that lead to it as well as many that miss it entirely. We can travel these roads, one after another if we wish. There is time. There is plenty of time. You don't even have to live a thousand years to do it. A normal lifetime—even a few years of dedication—will suffice. There is time. And if we were to go down those many roads, would there not be something to learn from each of them? Would we not, depending on our receptivity, become better for the journeys? I would like to think so. I am speaking, of course, of studying the great works of literature. With these books as guides, we can indeed comprehend much about the human condition in a fraction of the time it would take us on our own, were we relying on personal experience only. In fact, it would not be a stretch at all to say that reading the great works of literature can serve, all by itself, as an excellent education for life. Of course, there are other disciplines and much to learn from them as well, but there is nothing that addresses the whole of what it means to be human—intellect, emotions, and will—quite so well as a great piece of literature.

Obviously this is only one idea of many possible ones for the exordium. The key is that the communicator make a pointed attempt to both engage and entice. Without those effects on the audience, the communication is lost before it really begins.

Step Nine: *Choose and write a conclusion (peroratio).*

In a speech, you can always start the conclusion with a summary of the main points from the speech's body. In longer essays, this technique is helpful for the reader as well. But a summary of the main points covered should not be the very last words of the essay or the speech. Ideally, the communicator will find something here that will imprint itself emotionally on the consciousness of the audience, for emotions linger in a way that pure reasoning often does not. In this case, one might appeal to some of the emotions a reader of great literature will experience by way of the stories themselves:

Imagine the joy that settles over a reader when a favorite character, at the end of some long struggle, is released from it and stumbles, wounded but alive, into a new awareness, a new understanding of what all that prior pain was for. And if the character's life happens to be anything like the reader's, imagine the intensification of that joy, the vicarious apprehension of a truth that has, to that point, remained hidden but now offers itself in shining simplicity to be plucked like a daisy of the soul. To the attentive reader, literature has this kind of power. It's the power of life, with all its joys and sorrows, all its pleasures and pains, its victories and defeats, its lessons and its loves. Everything an education for life could hope to impart. There waiting for the student who aims to live.

Step Ten: *Create smooth transitions throughout.*

A crucial step for the cohesion of a piece of communication is to see that there are language links between the ideas so that the audience may follow, without disruption, the flow and sequence of the communicator's thought. A good group of words to keep in mind for this task are the various conjunctions: coordinating, subordinating, and adverbial. These connecting words help the audience to see different types of relationships between pairs of thoughts, whether it's to show similarity, contrast, concession, enumeration, exemplification, elaboration, cause, effect, conclusion, and so on. The lists that follow are not meant to be exhaustive but should give you an idea of what's available to the communicator when trying to make clear and smooth the movement from one thought to another.

Coordinating Conjunctions

Coordinating conjunctions (cc) are the most commonly used connectors of thought—so common, in fact, that we hardly notice them, yet their role is crucial. There are only seven in the English language: *and, but, for, nor, or, so,* and *yet.* Typically they are used, with the help of a comma, both to separate independent clauses (IC) and to show how those two clauses are related, as follows:
IC , cc IC.

Subordinating Conjunctions

Subordinating conjunctions (sc) initiate dependent clauses (DC) that have an adverbial influence on the independent clause to which they are attached, as follows:

sc DC , IC.
IC sc DC.

Here are some common subordinating conjunctions: *after, although, as, because, before, even though, if, once, since, so that, unless, until, when, whenever, where, whereas, wherever,* and *while.*

Conjunctive Adverbs

Effective use of conjunctive adverbs (ca) can go a long way toward helping a listener or a reader understand the flow of thought in a piece of communication. They can be used, with the help of a semicolon, both to separate independent clauses and to show relationships between them, as follows:

IC ; ca, IC.

They can also be used at or near the start of a new sentence (S.):

ca, S.

Here are some common conjunctive adverbs: *accordingly, actually, after all, also, anyway, as a result, besides, by contrast, certainly, consequently, conversely, first...second...third...etc., for example, for instance, furthermore, granted, hence, however, in addition, in fact, in other words, in short, incidentally, indeed, instead, likewise, meanwhile, moreover, naturally, nevertheless, next, nonetheless, on the contrary, on the other hand, rather, regardless, similarly, specifically, still, that is to say, therefore, thus,* and *ultimately.*

Appendix

Appendix

Following are two pieces of communication—an essay and a speech—that illustrate the use of classical oration as an organizing principle. A good exercise for the student of rhetoric would be to identify the various components—*exordium, narratio, partitio, confirmatio, refutatio, peroratio*—as well as the *thesis* and any transitional words or phrases in each sample.

Sample Essay

The Mercy of Limits

"It is not good to be too free. It is not good to have everything one wants."
~ Blaise Pascal

Who among us would turn down unlimited freedom if it were offered? Who would deny himself anything he wanted if all such things were available for the taking? Apparently Blaise Pascal might, or at least he might wish to, and there is good reason to believe that he might advise us to wish the same. After all, unlimited personal liberty would lead inexorably to unlimited ambition and acquisition, and that path is a black hole that, taken to its logical conclusion, would destroy not only ourselves but everything and everyone around us as well.

Although unlimited freedom has a strong instinctual appeal to the individual, it is, upon further consideration, not so good for everyone around him. Wherever there is community, then the complete freedom of one member is sure to infringe, eventually, on the freedom of others. Take, for instance, the community of the family. If one child exercises his freedom to play his stereo loudly all night long, then his siblings (not to mention his parents) are restrained from exercising their freedom to sleep. In such a case, there is only one person who is experiencing absolute freedom and perhaps several who are experiencing a limitation of their freedom. So the idea that unlimited freedom is an intrinsic good is very subjective. What is perceived as a good by one person (or even a few people) may in fact be perceived as a "bad" by one or more others. Living harmoniously in community therefore requires some voluntary restraint on one's own freedoms so that an equitable balance of freedoms may be experienced by all who live there. Thus, "it is not good to be too free" if the exercising of that freedom ends up thwarting the well-being of others.

But what about a hermit? Since he lives not in community, why should his freedom be restricted in any way? If a man eats an entire chocolate pie by himself and therefore deprives his family members of their dessert, he has exercised his freedom to the detriment of others, but if a hermit eats an entire chocolate pie in one sitting, what's the harm? After all, he has not deprived anyone else of dessert. Nevertheless, in this case, the harm he does is to himself. In all likelihood, he will suffer a stomach ache after such gluttony. But even if he has a cast-iron stomach, one that never feels regret for over-indulgence, his body will bear the effects of too much sugar all at once. Whether they are consciously felt immediately or not, there are indeed physiological consequences for such acts (i.e. the digestive process is slowed, insulin levels are raised, the immune system is depressed, and so on). Our hermit may have wanted very much to eat the whole pie, but "it is not good to have everything one wants," as Pascal well knew.

Some may object: if I want to eat the whole pie and am willing to suffer the consequences, that is my choice. Well, true enough, but that doesn't make it a "good" choice. It is an inherent bad to be sick, an inherent bad to do damage— however quietly—to one's own body, so while a person might have the freedom to choose poorly, doing so certainly does nothing to justify absolute freedom-of-choice as a good thing, and this is Pascal's point. Just because we want something doesn't mean we should.

So is he saying that all freedom is bad? Hardly. Freedom, kept within its proper bounds, is part of human nature and a wonderful thing. It is the gateway to many fine pleasures in life, from appreciating good music to eating good pie. Sometimes, though, we want things that are bad for us or for those around us, or both. It is then that freedom would be better restrained than indulged. So what Pascal is really saying is that *wanting* something is not, in and of itself, a good justification for getting it. He would say that our wants—our passions or desires—are of a lower order than our intellect. Or to put it another way, our intellect is capable of seeing consequences that our passions ignore (like what too much sugar will do to our bodies over the long term).

If then our free will is directed mostly or solely by the passions, we will sometimes step into "too much" freedom and likely suffer the consequences. If, on the other hand, our free will is directed by the intellect (or, in some cases, by faith in something even higher than human intellect), then freedom is kept in check, steered toward that which is truly good, both for ourselves and for those around us. There is no limit, in other words, on the freedom to do good, and Pascal surely would agree. What he warns us about, rather, is an unlimited freedom of the passions: It is not good to have *everything* one *wants*.

In the final analysis, it makes sense that such a quotation should come from Pascal, a philosopher and a Catholic. As a philosopher, he knew that the intellect is a trustworthy guide for finding truth. As a Catholic, he knew that divine revelation is higher even than the intellect. And on both counts, he knew that unrestrained satisfaction of personal desires is a dangerous path. Thank goodness, in other words, for limits.

Sample Speech

Literature for Life

Although we are each given only one earthly existence, I am here to say that it is possible nonetheless to live many lives, to see the world through multiple lenses and thus to understand it—and ourselves—better. Despite the fact that truth itself is one, there are many ways of finding it, many roads that lead to it as well as many that miss it entirely. We can travel these roads, one after another if we wish. There is time. There is plenty of time. You don't even have to live a thousand years to do it. A normal lifetime—even a few years of dedication—will suffice. There is time.

I am speaking, of course, of studying the great works of literature. With these books as guides, we can indeed take in much what it means to be human in a fraction of the time it would take us on our own, relying on solely personal experience. In fact, it would not be a stretch at all to say that reading the great works of literature can serve on its own as an excellent education for life. Of course, there are other disciplines and much to learn from them as well, but there is nothing that addresses the whole person—the intellect, the emotions, and the will—quite so deeply or so well as a great piece of literature.

And this is really at the core of a liberal arts education: to address the *whole* person. Incidentally, by liberal arts here, I do not mean *liberal* in the political or moral sense. Rather, I mean it in its traditional educational sense, as in the seven liberal arts, the study of which should have the effect of *liberating* the mind of the student, of setting it free by increasing its powers to reason, to understand, and to communicate well what is understood. Great literature aids us in this process, and insofar as it does, is a special branch of rhetoric, one that persuades and instructs indirectly through artifice and example.

In the following minutes, I hope to convince you that great literature can indeed accomplish this feat of education in our lives. We'll take a look at what is meant by a good education in general and mention some of the dangers one might face without it. Then we'll highlight a few famous examples from literature. And finally, we'll address the notion that "book learning" is not really necessary, the idea that experience, all by itself, can make us equally well educated.

Before we can say much about literature's role in education, we must first ask ourselves what a truly good education is. In his classic work, *The Idea of a University*, John Henry Newman describes the effects on a student of a strong liberal arts education. He says, and I quote,

> He profits by an intellectual tradition, [...] He apprehends the great outlines of knowledge, the principles on which it rests, the scale of its parts, its lights and its shades, its great points and its little, as he cannot otherwise apprehend them. Hence it is that his education is called 'Liberal.' A habit of mind is formed which lasts through life, of which the attributes are, freedom, equitableness, calmness, moderation, and wisdom.

"A habit of mind," says Newman, with the effects of "freedom, equitableness, calmness, moderation, and wisdom." Sounds like the conditions necessary for a well-lived life, does it not?

Yet it would be impossible to live as Newman describes without a deep understanding of human nature. How can we be *calm* or *wise*, for instance, if we do not understand our fellow man, where he is coming from, why he behaves the way he does? Imagine, for instance, someone who ignores human nature altogether, both in himself and in others. He will remain ignorant, it would be safe to say, of how his actions affect those around him, of his own motivations, of the motivations of others, and so on. It is likely that his life will be marked by impulsive behaviors, by a kind of slavery to his whims and his vices, by failed relationships, by an inconsistency of actions, in short by foolishness. Quite the opposite of those steady, measured traits that Newman names in association with a truly good education.

So it seems clear that a true education will include, and in fact is dependent on, a deep understanding of human nature. Now, where among the fields of study can we learn about human nature? Why, in literature, of course!

Consider Homer's *Odyssey*, where we learn about the human capacity for cunning, about the instinct for home and homewardness, about the desire for glory, the distraction of pleasure, the contrast of fidelity and infidelity, the suddenness of violence and vengeance, and so on.

Consider Cervantes' *Don Quixote*, where we learn about the human capacity for delusion, about the idealist's awkward journey through the realist's world, about relentless deception and ultimate redemption.

Or how about Shakespeare's *Hamlet*, where we learn about the human capacity for betrayal motivated by ambition, about the desire for justice coupled with the urge to avenge, about the strength of loyalty, the pain of grief, the paralysis between duty and fear, about madness in the face of abandonment, and about the spiritual instinct that persists in the soul.

I could go on and on, of course. Every great work of literature offers us a rich canvas of shapes and colors that speak to us in vivid detail of what it means to have human existence. And every time we read attentively one of these great works, we both broaden and deepen our understanding of the humanity that they illustrate. But this raises a question. There are those who might object that human nature can be learned—and learned better, perhaps—in places other than books. They might say, "Instead of reading about human life, why not simply live one and learn by experience?"

To this objection, I would reply that the reading of literature is not being proposed as a *substitute* for living your life. You still have to live your life, and in so doing, you may indeed learn certain things by experience, and that is to be desired, if we value learning at all. But the romantic notion of learning only by experience is not the rosy path to knowledge that some would make it out to be.

First, there can be some hidden costs. Learning by trial and error, without much understanding of human nature, can lead to naïve or self-absorbed decisions in financial matters, in matters of friendship and love, not to mention matters of physical health. And these mistakes can be costly. Second, experiential learning is limited in scope to one's own life, while learning through literature is virtually unlimited. There is always a new work to be taken up or an old one to be reread. And the overlap or repetition of certain ideas only serves to deepen them in your heart and mind. Living by experience alone offers nowhere near such volume of opportunity. And not only volume, but speed. One can live one's own life only at that unalterable pace. But in the space of a few years, one can also read a multitude of books in which a multitude of characters reveal a plenitude of human life. So there is a time advantage to the reading of great literature as well.

Just to be clear, I am not saying that experiential learning is worthless. Quite the contrary, it is a natural good, completely unique to each individual's set of personal circumstances. It is the primary means of instruction and an excellent one as far as it goes. But it only goes so far, and the serious study of great literature offers an exponential expansion on that inherent limit.

So, what have we covered, and what can we conclude? A good education ought to lead to a well-lived life. But what would a well-lived life look like? According to Cardinal Newman, it would include a formed habit of mind, "of which the attributes are, freedom, equitableness, calmness, moderation, and wisdom." And these, it is obvious to see, require a deep understanding of human nature. So something about a good education must provide for the willing student a deeper understanding of humanity. And that's where the study of literature is invaluable. Though we may learn much by experience, experience alone cannot teach with the speed or scope of literature. Not to mention that the costs of experience—financial and otherwise—can also be formidable as compared to the price of a book and the time it takes to read it closely.

Imagine the joy that settles over a reader when a favorite character, at the end of some long struggle, is released from it and stumbles, wounded but alive, into a new awareness, a new understanding of what all that prior pain was for. And if the character's life happens to be anything like the reader's, imagine the intensification of that joy, the vicarious apprehension of a truth that has, to that point, remained hidden but now offers itself in shining simplicity to be plucked like a daisy of the soul. To the attentive reader, literature has this kind of power. It's the power of life, with all its joys and sorrows, all its pleasures and pains, its victories and defeats, its lessons and its loves. Everything an education for life could hope to impart. There waiting for the student who aims to *live*.

About the Author

Michael Larson teaches English at Minnesota State College – Southeast Technical, in Winona, Minnesota. He is the author of *A Concise Guide to Documentation: MLA, APA, and Chicago*, as well as a book of poems, *What We Wish We Knew*, and a chapbook of poems, *The Light Remaining*. Mr. Larson is also the recipient of a National Endowment for the Arts fellowship in poetry, a Loft-McKnight fellowship in poetry, and an Iowa State Arts Board grant in fiction. A fly-fishing enthusiast and an occasional tournament chess player, he lives on an acreage near Winona with his wife and three children.

Made in the USA
Columbia, SC
20 July 2022

63774912R00052